For Johnnet +

lots of love

Nick

xxx

YOU CAN
CHOOSE
YOUR FRIENDS...

THE SIX KEY SKILLS THAT TURN
BUSINESS RELATIONSHIPS INTO RESULTS

NICK SAUNDERS

RE

First published in Great Britain 2017
by Rethink Press (www.rethinkpress.com)
© Copyright Nick Saunders

Cover image © macrovector / Freepik

PRAISE

"As work pressures increase, it's never been more important for colleagues to collaborate. Nick Saunders really helped our teams unlock the secrets to working together better. I recommend *You Can Choose Your Friends...* to anyone who wants to be a better leader or team player. It's also a highly entertaining read!"

Alex Alder, Customer Insights Director, Barclays UK

"How refreshing to find someone who really understands people, and can explain what they know so the rest of us can understand it too. If you apply the lessons in this book, they will make your life easier, more enjoyable and more successful."

Richard Templar, author of The Rules series

"You can choose your friends, and you can choose which business books to read. Just make sure you choose this one!"

Bob Boxer, Global Business Director, JWT

"Nick Saunders writes with the same clarity, wit and passion that he brings to his keynote speaking. *You Can Choose Your Friends...* is full of excellent advice and insight on how to get the best out of your workplace relationships, all presented in a practical and memorable way."

Frank Althaus, Author and Founder of Russian Language Centre

"About time – a self-help book which is engaging, amusing and informative! *You Can Choose Your Friends...* is an excellent guide to developing and nurturing relationships in the workplace with the key aim of driving success... and it works!"

Sophie Robinson, Commercial Support Manager, Pfizer UK

"Nick's unique blend of business thinking and rich real-life experience is wise, insightful and authentic. *You Can Choose Your Friends...* is a book that encapsulates all this."

Matt Dickinson, Author and Correspondent, The Times

"Having worked with Nick, I can speak from experience that his book exudes the same passion and energy that he does in person. *You Can Choose Your Friends...* is written from the heart and is practical, readable and relevant".

Alexandra Delamain, Snr Vice President – Global Head of Financial Services, The Economist

"Relationships matter in everything we do. *You Can Choose Your Friends…* is a book that will engage and educate everyone from a CEO running a multinational corporation to a teenager struggling with friendship issues. It's easy to pick up but with huge impact on every interaction you have with another human being. Nick is humorous and absolutely on the money yet again. A book I will be using and sharing across the education sector."

Benedick Ashmore-Short, Director of Education Primary
Reach4, 2014 Primary Headteacher of the Year

"You have to read this book. It is funny, thought provoking and incredibly helpful for anyone interested in improving relationships to produce better results. Follow Nick's advice, take the actions he suggests and your relationships at home, at work, wherever you are, will improve instantly."

Ali Stewart, Author, Executive & Leadership Coach,
Ali Stewart & Co Ltd

"I've been privileged to know Nick Saunders (and his family) for almost 30 years, and in my career in journalism and broadcasting, I've seldom met a better communicator. *You Can Choose Your Friends…* reflects his instinctive talent for connecting with people, and contains smart, practical and inventive insights into how to motivate and manage."

Paul Kelso, Broadcaster and Journalist, Sky News

For Dad

CONTENTS

ABOUT NICK – AND HIS FAMILY   1

INTRODUCTION   7

GETTING ON WITH EVERYONE   11

THE SIX KEY SKILLS TO WINNING OVER ANYONE   27

PAUSE   35

LISTEN AND LEARN   51

ADAPT   69

BE AUTHENTIC   87

BE HUMOROUS   103

BE GRATEFUL   117

TO SUM UP   137

ABOUT NICK – AND HIS FAMILY

*With my wife, Helen, and
our son, Luke*

For the past twenty-five years, I have been lucky enough to enjoy a career doing what I love.

As a professional speaker, training consultant and mentor, I've had the privilege of helping individuals enjoy and thrive in their careers by giving them practical tools to make their working lives happier and more successful.

I'm known as The Family Man because my experience has shown me that workplaces are like the family home: they both come with the same challenges, issues, niggles and frustrations. In this book, I punctuate my advice for a more harmonious and productive work life with examples of issues in my own family life to make it personal and, above all, relatable.

I don't dispense acres of bland general advice or mountainous off-putting step-by-step processes. I don't do management-speak, use high-brow lingo or make ludicrous claims about building a new planet or becoming a tiger. What I do best is empower people to get on with anyone and everyone – and I have the results to prove it.

I have helped improve relationships in all sorts of organisations and industries around the world.

For example:

- I coached a senior Relationship Director at Europe Arab Bank, helping him adapt his communication style when dealing with a challenging client. Result – a successful transaction earning the bank over £2million net income

- I ran a sales training programme in the USA for Fantech Systemair, a leading global supplier of energy efficient air climate solutions, which resulted in $500k increase in sales within fourteen days

- I have been working with Pfizer, the world's No. 1 pharmaceutical company, for sixteen years, developing and delivering over 100 management and leadership training interventions

- I led a programme with BUPA's Member Services Department, successfully improving customer retention by 20%

- I completed a leadership programme for Red Funnel, the well-known ferry company, resulting in a highly motivated management team who guided the business to an increased 15% market share within twelve months.

When in front of an audience, I challenge them to change and I get them to laugh. People often tell me they come away inspired – motivated to make a change and *do* something about it. And I'd love you to have the same experience when you read this book.

I'm a Londoner who loves wine, food, football, comedy, autobiographies, music (from Madness to Mozart) and the company of my family and close friends. In order to counter the food and wine bit, I keep fit, sometimes taking it to extreme lengths like completing the ultra-event *Marathon des Sables*, a gruelling race consisting of running six marathons in six consecutive days in the Sahara. (Did I mention I was competitive?)

I put any success I may have had down to the entire Saunders family, especially my wife, Helen, and my son, Luke. My two best mentors, they remind me daily that I'm not as great as I sometimes think I am.

And they're right.

INTRODUCTION

Getting on with people at work is paramount. It allows you to get the job done.

You will almost certainly know someone who is brilliant with people; someone who gets on with *everyone* they meet – a colleague, a teacher, your old boss. They have the talent to win over absolutely anybody. But here's the question – how do they do it? What specific things do they do to get on with and influence others successfully?

Chances are you'll come up with a good list, but producing the definitive list that *always* works isn't easy. But I believe I know the answer.

I believe there is a specific set of six skills, used by those who are the best at personal interactions to oil the wheels of work and get the job done. And I believe this because I was taught these six skills by a highly successful man who was simply brilliant at getting on with everyone he came into contact with. I saw how he employed the skills over the years and how they worked time and time again.

This man was, in fact, my father.

The good news is the six skills are simple, powerful and you almost certainly know them already. But knowing them is pointless if you don't use them to good effect. They require application and hard work.

When I go into businesses and organisations, I show people how to use these skills to enable them to work together better and get teams functioning more effectively. And I see that when people embrace the six skills and use them, the results are always the same: better relationships, better teamwork, better cooperation, better collaboration – all of which lead to better performance and increased profits.

The six skills turn relationships into results. In this book, I'm going to show you how to use them effectively.

CHAPTER 1

GETTING ON WITH EVERYONE

*"Happiness is having a large, loving,
caring, close-knit family... in another city."*

—

George Burns

I believe workplaces are like families. They are both made up of different personalities with different needs and different priorities. Most of the time, we get on fine with our colleagues and our families.

But obviously things can get a bit testing, a bit challenging, a bit demanding, both at home and at work. Sometimes we'll have people telling us what to do, not listening to us, being uncooperative, difficult, doing things their way, not our way. In these situations, especially when we're forced together over a period of time, such as families at Christmas, or work colleagues toiling eight to ten hours a day under pressure to deliver results, friction can surface. And that's when we can fall out.

MEET MY FAMILY

Now, I love my family. I love my wife, my son, Mum, Dad, my brothers, nephews, nieces, cousins – all of them. I'd literally lay down my life to save theirs. My heart bursts with pride when I think of them. I feel fortunate and privileged to be part of this family.

The Saunders Family

However, sometimes, just sometimes, *they drive me mental!*

Like at Christmas.

Christmas with my family always starts well, but by mid-morning on Boxing Day, I could easily take them back to the shop for a refund – along with the Christmas jumper and socks.

And it nearly always begins to go wrong in the kitchen. For starters, I've got my mum telling me how to turn the oven on. Now, when I turn on the oven, I like to whack it up to the maximum temperature, then reduce it to the required temperature once it's heated up. But Mum decides to give me a lecture about how the oven doesn't get hot any quicker if I whack it on full and I should just turn it to the correct temperature in the first place. OK, she has a point, but – it's my oven! I'm 54 years old and I own my own oven! She then shoos me away from the oven with her hands as if I'm still five years old.

Right, so I step away from the oven, sighing slightly, and go to stack the dishwasher. At this point, my brother arrives, telling me off because, apparently, the cutlery shouldn't be placed in the dishwasher facing down.

Fine! I was only trying to help. I'll go and stir the gravy (surely I can't go wrong here). But then my lovely wife, Helen, comes in.

'What are you doing? Get away from my gravy,' she says. 'Go and sort out the wine. And when we sit down to eat Christmas lunch, don't continually refill everyone's wine glass when they're still three quarters full like you did last year. Remember what happened to Granny.'

Of course, I *do* refill everyone's wine glasses (come on, it's Christmas), which backfires on me. Later in the day, Helen, who by this time is fairly merry, decides it's time to play her favourite song. Unfortunately for me, her favourite song is Westlife's 'You Raise Me Up' (no offence intended if you're a Westlife fan). Even worse, Helen plays it *five* times, back to back.

Arrrrrgggghhhhh!

And even Luke joins in. My gorgeous boy Luke, whom I'd do anything for, winds me up on Christmas Day.

Luke is thirteen years old, and boy, am I living the cliché of having a thirteen-year-old in the house.

How can my gorgeous boy go from this...

...to this?

'Luke.'

Silence.

'Luke?'

'Yea.' (Grunt.)

'Can you help me with a couple of things?'

(Humph.) 'It's Christmas Day. I just want to chill.' (Like he's had such a tough morning opening presents.)

'You can chill later. But for now I need you to help lay the table, then go upstairs and tidy your room.'

(Big sigh.) 'I'll do it later.'

'*Luke*, you won't do it later. I need you to do it now.'

'Oh, Dad, you're so needy!'

And he's right. I am needy. So is Luke, actually. And Helen. And you. And your kids. And your colleagues. And your boss. That's what it is to be human.

We all need things, but often different things. In that moment with Luke, he needed to chill, and I needed him to tidy his room.

Of course, you'll have your own needs in life. You might need success or money or knowledge. At the end of a long day, you might need a hug or exercise or a stiff drink – or all three!

The point is, it's hard to reconcile all our conflicting needs all the time. It's hard to be a parent, a spouse, a colleague and a boss.

THE COST OF CONFLICT

If this kind of conflict is allowed to build up it can lead to damaging relationships. At work, friction can cause hundreds, even thousands of problems – 30,614 problems, to be exact.

A 2014 report by Oxford Economics* revealed that on average, replacing an employee costs £30,614 in terms of advertising, lost output, agency fees and so on. Losing a member of staff because of conflict is expensive.

Oxford Economics is a venture set up with Oxford University's business college to provide economic forecasting and modelling to UK companies.

Conflict at work not only impacts individual companies, it also has a huge impact on the British economy. The same report by Oxford Economics cited that poor personal interactions cost the UK economy 40 million days in 2014. To put this figure into context, in the 1970s (the decade of strikes and the three-day week, when electricity would cut off suddenly and we'd sit around candles in the dark), the economy lost only 12.9 million days.

A report by the Chartered Institute of Personnel and Development (CIPD) published in 2015 looked at interpersonal friction at work and how this impacts on employees. It found that conflict was most common with line managers.

LEADING WITH EMPATHY

The world of business demands that we work together seamlessly. All of us need to be able to get on with, relate to, connect with and engage with people, especially if we are in a position of influence. Especially if we are in a position of leadership. The more senior you are, the more important it is to appreciate the impact your communication style can have on others.

A leader's primary function is to get work done through people. You might think, then, that the higher the position a person holds, the better their people skills. But it appears the opposite is true.

Too many leaders are promoted because of what they know or how long they have worked in an organisation, rather than for their skill in managing others. And once they reach the top, they actually spend less time interacting with staff.

A 2005 Harvard Business Review article, 'Heartless Bosses', measured the emotional intelligence (EQ) of half a million senior executives, managers and employees across industries on six continents with fascinating results. Those who had the highest EQ scores were the best performers. The research found that EQ skills were more important to job performance than any other leadership skill. And the fascinating bit was the higher the position a person held, the lower their EQ.

Of course, I'm not suggesting all bosses lack these skills. However, in my experience, bosses with a low EQ damage relationships rather than build them.

The worst type of boss can have a number of damaging behaviours, such as a tendency to discredit colleagues and their ideas, purporting to be more knowledgeable than others, avoiding blame and/or pinning blame on others, and ignoring feedback. All of these contribute to conflict at work.

Having worked with many leaders from businesses around the world, I've observed that being extremely intelligent is not enough. Yes, the best leaders do have a high IQ, but they also have a high EQ and the ability to empathise with anyone.

Sky CEO, Jeremy Darroch, says that empathy has overtaken more traditional business skills to become the most important requirement for leadership success.

> *A lot of the old skills of leadership aren't fit for the future. The idea that I can sit in the corner office and call the shots is long gone. Empathy is now the single most important skill when you get to the top of an organisation. It means you can frame opportunity and challenge in the right way.*
>
> — Jeremy Darroch

Darroch insisted all Sky's senior leaders undergo a year-long development programme centred around emotional intelligence.

> *It starts with me. When you're at the top you realise how vital you are to people. How I act, my mental state, my level of optimism, how I deal with stress and challenge, is fundamentally important to people.*
>
> — Jeremy Darroch

THE SCIENCE BIT

People who exhibit empathy and become attuned to others' moods literally effect both their own brain chemistry and that of people around them. Winning people over is less about mastering situations or social skills, and more about developing a genuine interest in fostering positive feelings in them.

The idea that leaders need to have social skills is not new. In 1920, psychologist Edward Thorndike said, 'The best mechanic in a factory may fail as a foreman for lack of social skills.'

MIRRORING EMOTIONS

Neuroscientists have identified mirror neurons in the brain. When we consciously or unconsciously detect someone else's emotions through their actions, our mirror neurons reproduce those emotions.

In a study conducted by Professor Marie Dasborough, one group of individuals received negative feedback accompanied with positive signals – nods and smiles. A second group received positive feedback delivered critically with frowns and narrowed eyes. It was proved that the first group felt much more positive on receiving good natured negative feedback than the second group, who had received positive feedback delivered negatively. Therefore, the delivery was more important than the message itself.

It has also been shown that there's a subset of mirror neurons whose only job is to detect other people's smiles and laughter, prompting smiles and laughter in return. A boss who is self-controlled and humourless will rarely engage those neurons, but a boss with an easy-going nature and sense of humour will trigger similar reactions in others, resulting in people taking in information more effectively and responding quickly and creatively.

Herb Kelleher, co-founder and CEO of Southwest Airlines in the USA, would wander around Dallas Airport offering beaming smiles, shaking hands with customers and saying how he appreciated their business. He also made the effort to thank employees for their hard work personally. He got back what he gave – his staff loved him. The business was known to have extremely high morale and low staff turnover.

THE BENEFITS OF GREAT COLLABORATION

The value of getting on well with everyone is huge. How would your organisation benefit if there were fewer rows, clashes, frayed tempers? Destructive conflict doesn't solve problems – it contributes to them.

Benefits that result from great communication and collaboration might include:

- Better internal decision making

- Solving problems and rapid innovation

- More efficient working

- Influencing the FD to get that extra resource

- Enhanced job satisfaction

- Improved employee retention

- Focusing the team on the vision of the business

- Persuading the MD to hold on planned cutbacks

- Winning over the Board with a new marketing strategy

- Selling an idea to senior decision makers

- Fewer misunderstandings/more productive meetings

- Stronger cross-functional working between teams.

Collaborative leaders are open to input, different viewpoints and constructive debate.

So who do people think of as great collaborators?

Barack Obama is acknowledged as being an excellent collaborator. As President of the USA, he was able to motivate the different departments at the White House to work together and cooperate fully to drive through policies. On a personal level, Obama has a reputation for staying calm and seeking a collaborative solution to issues, rather than trying to force through a resolution.

Alessandro Carlucci, Brazil's Natura Cosmeticos CEO, instigated a comprehensive 'engagement process' to promote a collaborative mindset and help win the firm a top spot on Fortune's list of best companies for leaders. Each leader in the firm had to disclose some personal life history, showing their vulnerability and including examples of failures, proving that they don't have all the answers. Business grew by 21% in 2010, and the collaborative mindset at the top cascaded down to the rest of the organisation.

> *Apple look to employ wicked people, smart people, people who don't care who gets the credit, who appreciate different points of view, share ideas and are happy for others to push the idea further and get the credit for it. The magic is in the collaboration.*
>
> — Tim Cook, current CEO at Apple

IT'S ALL ABOUT PEOPLE

So all of us should aim to be great collaborators, striving to get on with and engage with anyone and everyone. But that doesn't mean walking around holding hands and dancing off into the sunset of eternal happiness. I mean there must be a sensible, professional, effective way to get on with, cooperate with, collaborate with people – while not necessarily *liking* everyone.

Having worked for twenty-five years in the corporate world, delivering hundreds of sessions, I have observed:

- 100% of employees are *people*
- 100% of colleagues are *people*
- 100% of clients are *people.*

When I go into a business, there is one question I ask everyone I meet: 'What's the best thing about your job?' And in the top three answers is always 'The people'. When I go into a business and ask everyone I meet, 'What's the *worst* thing about your job?', in the top three answers is always (yes, you know what's coming) 'The people'.

It doesn't really matter how great your research, product or marketing is. Ultimately the success of any organisation is pretty much down to people interacting with people. If you don't get on with people, you won't get on in business. If you can't collaborate with people, you won't *have* a business. In today's fast-changing global environment, it's vital to get people working together seamlessly across departments, functions and geographic boundaries.

And that's precisely what I do. I work with organisations, businesses, companies, charities, schools, getting teams functioning more effectively to improve performance and increase profit.

And how do I do that? By teaching the six skills.

RECAP
GETTING ON WITH EVERYONE

1. Workplaces are like families with different personalities and priorities

2. The success of any organisation is down to people interacting well with people

3. When forced together, of course we fall out from time to time

4. Everyone has different needs; it's hard to reconcile these conflicting needs

5. It's not about liking everyone – it's about collaborating with them.

CHAPTER 2

THE SIX KEY SKILLS TO WINNING OVER ANYONE

It is vital to get on with people. While I think I've managed to relate to most people at home and at work, I still found some people difficult to deal with. I came to the conclusion that I needed to improve the way I communicated with everyone around me, both at home and at work.

I needed guidance, help, an answer. And I started looking all over the place – books, articles, mentors. They all helped, but I felt there was more to learn. I knew I didn't yet have the answer.

Like a lot of things, the answer was close to home. But sometimes when things are right there in front of you, you don't see them. My answer came from someone who was an expert at winning over people, someone who was outstanding at getting on with everyone he met. He was the most agreeable, like-able person I've ever met... and he happened to be my Dad.

THE MASTER

My father was a giant 6ft 6in teddy bear of a man. He was friendly, funny, playful, cheeky; full of life and easy going; loved messing around and playing the joker. He was generous with his time, his spirit and his compliments. Everyone liked and respected him – he had a knack with people.

He was one of life's good 'uns.

With Dad   *With Dad, forty years later*

But by no means was he just the playful fool. He was an outstanding surgeon and had a distinguished career, becoming Vice President of the Royal Society of Medicine and working with the highest in the land.

Dad having a chat with You Know Who

During his career, not only did he get on with the thousands of patients he treated, making them feel relaxed and comfortable in his company, he also got on with all his colleagues (no mean feat in the rarefied medical world full of egos).

Indeed, a colleague said of Dad, 'Peter Saunders is the only doctor I know who has no enemies in the medical world.'

So, there I was looking for answers to the question of how to improve my relationships with the people in my life, and right in front of me was my Dad – the best mentor, the best role model I could ever find.

Of course, you don't appreciate what you've got until it's taken away from you. In late 2003, Dad was diagnosed with cancer and given only months to live.

As any of you who have faced the prospect of losing someone close to you will know, this re-focuses the mind somewhat. Subsequently, Dad and I had many delightful, heartfelt, emotional conversations, and one centred on what made him the man he was. I wanted to know, in his words, what he did to be so liked, so popular, so respected.

So, one evening in December 2003, I sat down with a frail but still mentally sharp Dad. I remember saying, 'Dad, I need to know.'

And I'll never forget that he grabbed my wrist, looked into my eyes, and said, 'Nick, you're so needy!' And then he laughed. 'But fortunately, you have everything you need.'

I didn't really understand what he meant by that and he noticed I looked confused. So he grabbed a pen and paper and drew a picture.

'Right, Nick,' he said to me, 'this is what it takes to get on with anyone and everyone.'

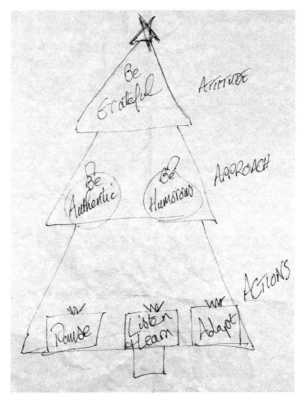

Dad's drawing

It is a Christmas tree, apparently. My dad was a brilliant man, but not a brilliant artist, although he was very proud of his drawing at the time.

And his drawing is what this book is all about.

He said, 'At the bottom of the tree are three *Actions*. These are the things you need to *do* to get on with anyone, OK?'

He looked at me with raised eyebrows, waiting for an answer. I nodded.

'Above the three Actions are two *Approaches*. I'll come to those later.' He was already on his second glass of wine by now, so I wasn't quite sure exactly when 'later' would be. 'And at the top of the tree, I'm going to talk about *Attitude*. Three Actions, two Approaches and one Attitude. So the first Action is...'

In the following chapters, I'm going to show you how, with application and hard work, you can use these skills powerfully, helpfully and effectively so you can improve your relationship with anyone you come into contact with.

My tutor

RECAP
THE SIX KEY SKILLS TO WINNING OVER ANYONE

Three Actions

Two Approaches

One Attitude

CHAPTER 3
PAUSE

"I was always the kid at school who thought
it was a good idea to set off the fire alarm...
I wish I could just pause and go, 'Is this
really what you want to do?"

—

James Corden

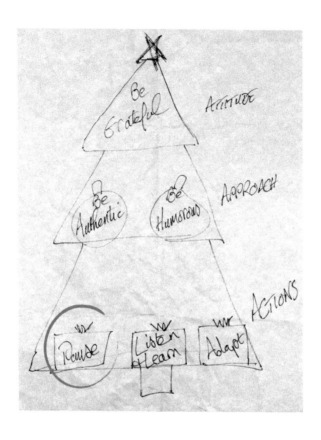

Be Grateful — ATTITUDE

Be Authentic   Be Humorous — APPROACH

Revise   Listen & Learn   Adapt — ACTIONS

'The first Action,' my dad said to me, 'the first thing you must do, Nick, whenever you are in front of someone, is... *pause*.

'Every time you meet someone, whether it's a formal conversation, a brief discussion, a casual chat, or a stressful exchange, pause. Because when you pause, you allow yourself to assemble your strategy for how best to deal with that particular situation.'

Dad thought that pausing was one of the most important things a human being can do. To illustrate his point, he told me a story which made me think about who we are as people.

'Imagine', he said, 'you're standing in a packed lift when someone behind you prods you in the back with an umbrella. You think nothing of it. But then it happens a second time. You ignore it again, but then it happens a third time. How do you feel? Now you're annoyed, but you say nothing.

'Then it happens for a fourth time. You spin around to say something, and there, right in front of you, is a blind guy trying to feel his way with his stick. *Now* how do you feel? *Now* what do you say?

'Naturally, your initial instinct was to yell, "What do you think you're doing?" But you have the ability to check your natural response – and you do that by *pausing*.'

LOGIC VS EMOTION

As a surgeon, my father understood how the body worked. He also understood the neurology of the mind, and he explained to me, in simple terms, that everything we see, hear, smell, taste and touch travels through our bodies in the form of electric signals. These signals pass from cell to cell until they reach the brain.

The signals enter the brain at its base near the spinal cord and travel to the frontal lobe behind the forehead, where our rational, logical thinking takes place. It's here where our brains make sense of all this information.

The thing is, before the signals reach the logical part of the brain, they pass through the limbic system along the way, and the limbic system is the place where our emotions are produced. So, we experience things *emotionally* before *reason* kicks in.

Throw in the fact that our emotional response is five times more powerful than our logical one and you can imagine the sheer strength of our emotions.

Dr Steve Peters, the well-known Consultant Psychiatrist, wrote the excellent book *The Chimp Paradox*. In it, he refers to the emotional part of the brain as 'the chimp'. We all have a chimp who is cheeky, independent and strong. So, in certain stressful situations, such as when your boss criticises you in front of your colleagues, the *logical* part of your brain might be saying, 'Listen to this criticism because it may prove useful in furthering your self-development', the *emotional* part is probably saying something very different.

Or how about when you're in a café, staring lovingly at a delicious piece of chocolate cake? Your *logical* response might say, 'You're on a diet, you'll only feel guilty later if you have it', but your *emotional* response might be, 'Stuff it. Life's too short!'

So, we have an ongoing battle between the emotional part of the brain and the logical part. However, all of us at some point in our lives have managed to keep our emotions in check, even though we may have been pushed very hard. How? By giving the logical part of the brain some time to catch up with the emotional part. We *pause*, take a breath before we react; before we do or say something we may regret. And when we pause, it inevitably leads to a better outcome.

In a previous role as Client Director, I remember working with colleagues, trying to close a significant piece of business with a tricky customer. He was demanding and dismissive in his attitude, but we really needed to make the deal.

At one point in the meeting, he made a rude comment

to my colleague, and I was about to react by saying something rather unprofessional (which would have undoubtedly lost the sale). Fortunately, I managed to pause, allowing my emotions to subside and the logical side take over.

Twenty minutes later, he signed the contract, which was worth £100k to the business. I learnt a big lesson that day – pause and stay cool.

THE CHRISTMAS SUPERMARKET SHOP

Of course, the difficult thing is *remembering* to pause in the heat of the moment, when the tension is rising and we're getting stressed. Personally, this is something I experience in particular once a year when I have to go with my wife Helen on the annual Christmas supermarket stock-up.

This jaunt around the aisles induces a particularly high degree of stress. Actually, I start to get stressed before we've even left the house, because I know what's coming. Then my stress levels rise as soon as we're in the car and hit major traffic. After what seems like for ever, we eventually arrive at the supermarket to find the car park full, so we spend fifteen minutes driving around with other stressed-out shoppers, desperately looking for a space. Naturally, this only adds to my anxiety.

Once in the supermarket, I just want to go to the beer and wine section, but no, I'm handed a list by my wife which contains eighteen different kinds of vegetable (half of which

I've never heard of). I'm sent to get enough cheese to feed an army, way too many sausages, three different types of brandy butter and a bottle of Christmas scented bleach. (Did you know there is such a thing as Christmas scented bleach?)

Finally, we've got everything and head to the till. The queues are enormous, so I am faced with the vitally important decision of choosing which queue to join. And of course, I choose the queue that doesn't move while the others are flowing beautifully.

Eventually, we get to the cashier and load up the shopping. Then Helen turns to me and says, 'Give me the vouchers.'

'What vouchers?'

'The vouchers. The £60 worth of vouchers I pointed to on the kitchen table as we left the house. The vouchers that I've been collecting for months.'

'I didn't see you point to any vouchers.'

'You didn't bring the vouchers?'

'No, I didn't bring the vouchers.'

'*What?* You're joking! You only have to remember to do one thing all Christmas, and you even mess that up. I do *everything* at this time of year for your bloody family.'

'I think you'll find it's "our" bloody family,' I say.

'Arrgghh!'

And off she storms, out of the store, leaving me at the checkout looking like an idiot...without any vouchers. People point at me, whispering to each other, 'He forgot the vouchers.'

If only Helen had paused. OK, if only *I'd* paused, too.

In that moment of stress, what we needed was a memory jogger – a reminder to pause – to allow time for the logical part of our brains to catch up with the emotional part.

So, next time you're in a difficult situation with someone and the tension's rising, remember to pause.

I worked closely with the CEO of a business in the City. Although he had a successful track record, his leadership style was fiery, direct and often aggressive. This side of his personality could be damaging – to the degree that over the course of eighteen months, he had lost three members of his leadership team. Replacing them cost his business over £200,000.

I spent several months coaching this highly intelligent, proud man, focusing on simple yet powerful techniques to help him pause and prevent his emotional side taking over. After some initial resistance, he worked hard at pausing, and although it took him some time, he reduced his emotional outbursts significantly and became less aggressive in his interactions.

> Two of his direct reports later confessed they had
> been planning to leave, but decided to stay because
> of the change in his conduct.

HOW TO PAUSE

So how do we pause? What things can we do to help us pause in those stressful moments?

There are many strategies that can help do this. The classics – take a deep breath, count to ten, etc. – can be effective. Here are some others to try:

Get in the helicopter

Imagine you're in a helicopter, hovering above the situation you're faced with. Look down and get some perspective on what's happening. How important is the situation? Will it last for ever? Think of all the critical things in your life. Is this really one of them?

Leave the room

If possible, distance yourself from the situation. Explain to the person that you would like some time out to think before you respond. If you can, leave the room.

Listen to the little voice

In stressful situations, the logical part of the brain will be trying to talk to you above the din of the emotional part – a little voice warning you to pause and not overreact.

> Here's a true story from someone I know very well.
> Some years ago, he was at Heathrow Airport, waiting

to fly on a business trip, and had time to kill. He decided to buy a book for the journey and visited a well-known book shop at the terminal. Browsing through the best-sellers, he found one and decided to buy it.

Turning around to head for the till, he saw a huge queue. Then he did something on the spur of the moment; something he'd never done before (or since, he assures me) – he turned and walked out of the shop with the book in his hand…without paying for it. He knew what he was doing was wrong, but ignored that little voice telling him so.

He felt guilty for a few seconds, but soon put it out of his mind. Once on the plane, he started reading. The book was a self-help guide, focusing on doing the right things in life, having dignity, being a good parent, helping others, being a good role model. By page 12, he felt pretty guilty. By page 26, he felt terrible.

It dawned on him that he was a common thief. He'd risked being caught, arrested and losing his job – all for a saving of £12.99 and avoiding waiting 5 minutes in a queue.

He decided to make up for it the best way he could. On returning from his trip, he wrote a letter to the author with a £50 note inside and bought five copies of the book to give to friends. The author wrote back thanking him and saying how amusing he found the story. He even told his wife.

If only my friend had listened to that little voice in his head at the airport, he'd have paused and not risked getting a criminal record.

BILL'S STORY

One of my previous jobs involved managing a group of twelve, each of whom had their own team. I remember watching one of my managers getting angry with a direct report (we'll call him 'Bill') for giving a sloppy, unclear presentation. The presentation had been confusing and unprofessional, but the way the manager responded – emotionally, aggressively, without pausing – damaged Bill's confidence. Indeed, Bill's next presentation was even worse.

I had a chat with the manager and we discussed what he could have done differently when criticising Bill. I stressed the importance of pausing before having the conversation to allow the logical side of the brain time to catch up with the emotional side. We talked about what he could have said if he'd thought about his words, and came up with:

'Bill, your presentation lacked structure and was unclear, which, in turn, left the audience confused. It needs to have absolute clarity from the beginning, be shorter and look more professional. Would it help if we talked through how you could improve it?'

No anger, no frustration, not even disappointment. Just an honest offer of support said in a calm, logical

> manner. Two weeks later, Bill delivered a superb
> presentation to the Board. That's the power of
> pausing.

Think of the consequences

This is not an easy strategy, but it's a powerful one. Pause in the moment of stress by thinking of *the consequences* of how you're about to react.

If we react emotionally, the chances are we'll do or say something we're likely to regret. The next day, we may reflect on how we behaved, having hurt someone and potentially damaged our relationship with them. As we're not robots, we'll almost certainly feel guilty, needing to apologise and face up to our actions.

But the damage is already done.

If we focus on the *consequences* of our reaction for a second or two before we open our mouth, we have a much better chance of preventing ourselves saying something we regret.

OVER TO YOU

Think about what happened the last time you reacted without pausing, at work or home. What were the consequences of your actions or words?

Jot down what you could have done differently to produce a better outcome.

RECAP
PAUSE

1. Pausing is one of the most important things a human being can do

2. We experience and feel things *emotionally* before *reason* kicks in

3. Our emotional response is five times more powerful than our logical side

4. To stop the emotional side taking over, we need to slow down the brain

5. Which strategy will you use to remember to pause?

CHAPTER 4
LISTEN AND LEARN

*'Bore' – noun. A person who talks
when you wish them to listen.*

—

Oxford Dictionary

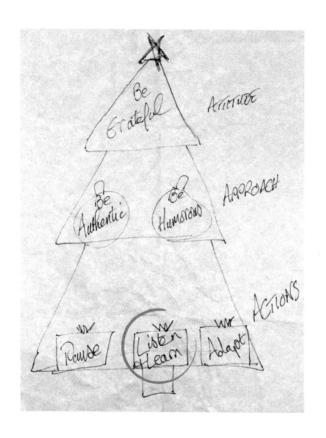

So, Dad's first Action was pause. And pausing leads on to the next Action.

Dad said, 'Having paused, you then need to assemble your strategy for how best to deal with the person and situation in front of you. And the most important things to do here are listen and learn. Work out who the person is and what they need.'

'If you want to get on with someone – anyone – you need to understand them, talk to them, ask questions. Listen to their answers, and the silence between their answers. Watch their body language, study them, be curious. Curiosity allows you to learn about someone and consequently build a strong relationship with them.'

There are some great quotes on this subject. My favourites include one from Atticus Finch in Harper Lee's *To Kill a Mockingbird*:

> *You never really understand a person until you consider things from his point of view… until you climb into his skin and walk around in it.*

And from Stephen Covey in his 25 million bestselling book *The 7 Habits Of Highly Effective People*:

If I were to summarize in one sentence the single most important principle I have learned in the field of interpersonal relations, it would be this: seek first to understand, then to be understood. This principle is the key to effective interpersonal communication.

In his book, Covey tells a story of travelling on the New York subway one Sunday morning. The carriage is peaceful and quiet as everyone is doing their own thing. But the tranquillity is shattered and the whole atmosphere changes when the train stops at a station and a father gets on with his three children.

The kids run around, shouting at each other, being generally disruptive. But the father just sits there with his eyes closed, oblivious. People are getting irritated that the man is taking no responsibility for his kids' behaviour.

After a while, Covey decides he has to say something.

'Excuse me, sir, your kids are disturbing a lot of people. Would you mind controlling them a little more?'

The father opens his eyes and says softly, 'I'm so sorry, you're right. I should do something about it. We've just come from the hospital where their mother died an hour ago.'

A powerful story.

BE CURIOUS

The key to relating to someone is not about what's happening in *your* world, but what's happening in *their* world. And to find that out, you need to be curious.

Ask questions and truly listen to what they have to say. When people realise that they're being heard, they'll tell you what's important to them – be it about their jobs, their dreams, their fears, their goals. Knowing what's important to them, you can connect with, relate to and interact with them. This is especially important at work, as it will give you perspective on how to do your job better.

So be curious.

QUESTIONS, QUESTIONS, QUESTIONS

When you ask someone questions, they need to be the *right* questions. Kids, being naturally inquisitive, are brilliant at asking questions. Often one of the first words to leave their lips is 'Why?' But as adults, we lose the art of asking bright, intelligent questions.

I have delivered literally thousands of training events on leadership, management skills, influencing skills, negotiation skills, sales and coaching. In every one of these programmes, I have included a session on questioning techniques.

It never ceases to amaze me how lacking most people are at the skill of questioning.

So what makes a good question? What questions work well?

Obviously, the right question depends on the situation you are facing. You may be coaching one of your team, influencing your boss, talking to a prospective client, seeking clarification from a colleague, selling a product or chatting to a friend about their weekend. Whatever the situation, the key to getting the right information is to ask the right questions.

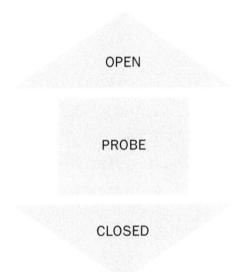

There are three main types of questions: open, probe and closed.

OPEN QUESTIONS

Open questions get the conversation flowing. These are used to get the other person to share information. We want them to talk about the things they want to talk about.

The important thing is to start an open question the right way. There are specific words to use.

For example: 'What are your thoughts on...?'; 'How do you see this developing? Why is that?'; 'Tell me about the situation with...'; 'Describe what happened when...'

PROBE QUESTIONS

Having started the conversation with an open question, often we will need more information to build on something the person has told us. This requires us to probe more deeply. Probing questions help us to get this supplementary information.

Open question: 'So how did the meeting go?'

'It went well. We got the information we needed from the client to move the project on.'

Probe questions: 'Tell me more about the information you got from the client'; 'How will this information ensure the project moves on?'; 'Which elements of the information you received are the most useful?'

Asking an open question is good but may only scratch the surface. In many situations, in order to understand the person/problem/issue, we may start with an open question but follow it up with a probe question.

CLOSED QUESTIONS

Closed questions are designed to get a one word answer – usually yes or no. Their purpose is to establish specific facts/information, clarify something or gain agreement.

They nearly always start with a verb. For example: 'Does that make sense?'; 'Are you OK with that?'; 'Have you got any concerns?'; 'Shall we go ahead?'

Closed questions play an important part in personal interactions, but be careful not to ask *too* many. Often people ask a closed question and get a one word reply when actually they were expecting a lot more.

QUESTIONS TO AVOID

- **Counterproductive questions,** for example: 'Why did you think I asked you to proofread it before we printed it?'

- **Leading questions,** for example: 'You don't really think that, do you?'

- **Multiple questions,** i.e. two or more questions presented as a package.

- **Marathon questions,** asked in a long, rambling, incomprehensible manner.

- **Ambiguous, vague or non-specific questions.**

- **Rhetorical questions:** a question that answers your own question.

As an executive coach working with high-powered CEOs, I've found that asking for information and feedback is often something that doesn't come naturally to them. But when CEOs hire and manage smart people who have more expertise in a certain area than they do, they have to ask, listen and learn.

The best CEOs use questions to evoke openness and curiosity rather than pre-determined answers. They ask with an interest in learning as opposed to judging.

One of my CEOs is superb at the art of questioning. He asks each member of his team, 'How can I help you to be successful?' about five times a day.

Another CEO I coach responds to a question from one of her team with a question of her own. She says, 'When someone comes to me with a problem, I often ask them, "If I had a magic wand to solve this problem, what would you want me to do with it?"'

THE TOP FIVE HABITS OF CURIOUS PEOPLE

To help you master the simple and highly effective skill of asking the right questions, here are the top five habits of the curious.

They listen without judgement

Many people make assumptions as they listen. Yet curious people have no hidden agenda. They seek to understand the perspectives of others without having a vested interest in the outcome.

They're present

Curious people focus 100% on the conversation they're having at that moment. If you're multitasking, you're not creating the right environment in which to be curious.

They're willing to be wrong

Curious people look at a broader array of options for solutions to problems. A workforce that feels valued will open up a resource of brilliant ideas, which will often improve results.

They make time

Curiosity needs to be intentional. It requires effort to put aside 'important stuff' and spend time on being curious, as the best solutions are often produced when people stop and ask, 'Why?'

They admit when they don't know

Curious people seek knowledge by engaging in conversations. When asked a question, they admit when they don't have an answer. It's more important for them to learn than to look smart.

I had a client who became the MD of a fabric manufacturer. He spent time getting to know the team on the production line, listening to their thoughts on what worked and what didn't. When the MD was talking to one softly spoken operative, the mechanic mentioned an idea to help solve a problem that had long hindered the manufacturing process. The MD thanked him for the suggestion and promised he'd look into it.

A couple of weeks later, the MD tried out the mechanic's proposed idea, and it worked. The MD was delighted and called him into his office.

'That was a great suggestion. When did you come up with the idea?'

'Thirty-two years ago,' the mechanic replied. 'No one ever asked me before.'

HOW TO LISTEN

Of course, it's no good being superb at asking great questions if you're no good at listening. The phrase 'I'm going to give him a damn good talking to' is commonplace, but how often do you hear the phrase 'I'm going to give him a damn good listening to'?

Excellent listening demands excellent levels of concentration. The two are directly connected. The more you concentrate, the better you listen.

The figure that follows illustrates this. The vertical axis measures our level of concentration; the horizontal axis measures how well we listen, giving us four levels of listening: Passive, Selective, Active and Evaluative.

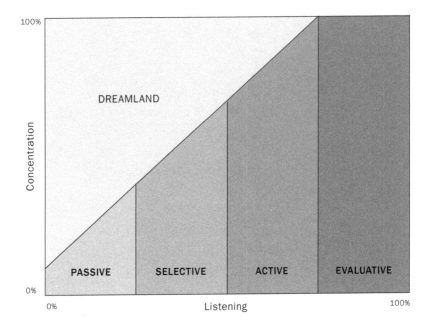

Passive listening is basically not listening. There may be sounds going on around us, but we don't hear them. They're not getting into our brain.

The next level of listening is what my wife accuses me of doing – a lot. **Selective listening** is when we *sort* of listen, but really we're choosing to listen to the bits we want to hear.

At the **Active level,** we are really listening to someone during a conversation. We're present, in the moment, ears open, paying attention, taking note of what's being said.

The final level of listening is one that we don't do enough – **Evaluative listening.** This is when the situation demands we concentrate to the maximum – a meeting with the boss; a chat with an important client; a job interview.

Evaluative listening is when we listen *and* think. We analyse and process what's being said and come up with questions.

'Are they making sense? Does their body language match their words? What are the consequences of what they're saying?'

We're making some decisions, some judgements.

Evaluative listening is listening to three specific things:

- **The content – what the person is actually saying**
- **Their emotion – frustration, anger, passion**
- **Their intent – what's really behind the words?**

You don't suddenly become an evaluative listener. You choose to do it, and it requires hard work.

OVER TO YOU

Try the quiz below by reading each statement and answering *true* or *false*.

When people talk to me:

I always give my undivided attention

I am never distracted by emails, the phone or other people

I never let my mind wander

I always give eye to eye contact

I never have to ask people to repeat things they have just told me

I tend to nod as I listen

I indicate understanding with 'Yes, right, I see' or their equivalents

I often take notes

I evaluate the message as I go along

I frequently summarise what's been said to confirm understanding

I deliberately ask relevant follow-on questions

How did you do?

That was a bit of fun, but it's real intention is to get you thinking about how good you are at listening. If you answered 'true' to all of them, I'll eat my hat!

I've been fortunate to work with some outstanding bosses. One quality they all possessed – without exception – was the ability to ask questions and listen to the replies.

My first boss was called Sue. She'd often call me into her office and say, 'Listen to this phone call.' Then she'd ask what I'd learnt from it before explaining the politics of what had just happened: I'd be expected to handle the next one.

Additionally, with each project she gave me, she'd ask loads of questions on how I thought I would deal with it. This not only helped me focus on the task, it also gave me immediate clarity on how I would tackle it.

I had another boss who, whenever I asked him a question, replied, 'What do you think?' He had the answers, but wanted me to learn. And I learnt more from him than just about any other manager.

RECAP
LISTEN AND LEARN

1. Assemble a strategy to deal with the person/situation best

2. Ask questions beginning with *tell me, describe, explain*

3. Be an Evaluative Listener – listen to people's answers

4. Watch their body language

5. Study them

6. Be curious.

CHAPTER 5

ADAPT

*"If there is any one secret of success, it lies in the
ability to get the other person's point of view and
see things from that person's angle."*

—

Henry Ford

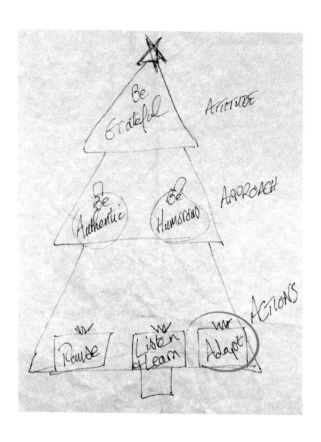

'So,' Dad continued, 'once you've paused, listened and learnt in order to understand the situation better than you did a moment ago, the next action is to *adapt*. Adapt your language, tone and style to one that is in harmony with the worldview of your new friend or colleague.'

We adapt all the time. Do we behave the same way with a client in a meeting, with friends or with the in-laws? Adaptation is a natural part of who we are. But the better we can adapt, the better our impact will be on the person we're talking to.

Dad was brilliant at adapting. As a doctor in front of his patients, he would pause, see the situation from their point of view to work out their underlying need, and then adapt his message accordingly. Everyone has something different they need or want. Some patients wanted reassurance that an upcoming operation would go well. Some wanted clarity of information regarding the operation. Some wanted reassuring that they had made the right choice to have the operation. Some wanted encouragement and support. Some just wanted a hug.

Dad felt it was his job – as important as the treatment – to find out what each patient's need was and give it to them as part of his communication style.

Dad - an expert at adapting

I worked with a senior director at Pfizer, the world's No. 1 global pharmaceutical company. Although demanding, he was superb with his people – particularly at adapting his communication style to match the particular situation he faced.

Based in the USA, he made it his business to spend time with his team, despite them being spread over the world. On one visit to the UK, he learnt of a colleague who had just returned to work following a terrible experience. She'd had complications while giving birth and lost her baby.

As soon as he heard this news, he cancelled two important meetings and went to see her, spending two hours chatting with her. Despite being a direct, hard-nosed man, he adapted his behaviour to reveal the sympathetic and supportive side of his nature. She was genuinely touched and impressed by this gesture, as was the whole team. They still talk about it in the office – five years on.

IDENTIFY A PERSON'S PERSONALITY

To adapt your communication style successfully in order to boost your chances of getting what you want when dealing with someone, you must first identify which personality type they are.

There are four distinct personality types. As I describe the traits of each one, you might think, *I work with a person like that*, or *I am married to someone like that*, or *that's my boss*, or *ooh, that's me!*

Of course, we humans are too complicated and sophisticated to be categorised as one particular personality type. We are a combination of all four types, and it's how we combine the four that makes us unique. However, one type will most accurately define us.

The four types are Direct, Sociable, Caring and Detailed.

DIRECT:

- Determined, strong willed, likes to be in control
- Approaches others in a straightforward manner
- Single-minded and focused on results
- Seeks outcomes that are specific and tangible.

SOCIABLE:

- Enthusiastic, persuasive, outgoing
- Wants to be involved
- Enjoys the company of others
- Likes to be noticed and appreciated for their contributions.

CARING:

- Patient, kind, relaxed, empathetic
- Looks for harmony and depth in relationships
- Good listener, considerate when making decisions
- Likes to be liked, uncomfortable in confrontational situations.

DETAILED:

- Cautious, formal, deliberate, questioning
- Reflects before speaking
- Values independence and wants to be correct
- Likes information to be accurate.

OVER TO YOU

If you had to put the four in order, from the type that best describes you to the one that least describes you, how would you rate them? Start with the type most like you at No.1.

1

2

3

4

HOW TO ADAPT

To connect with others better, you don't so much need to know your own personality type as work out theirs. You can often fathom this out from how people talk and act. Observe their mannerisms, their body language, how loud, quiet, energetic, calm they are.

Once you have worked out their main personality type, you can then adapt your communication style.

There are some Dos and Don'ts for communicating with each of the types.

DIRECT:

DO	DON'T
Cut to the chase	Go into too much detail
Talk about results/benefits	Discuss emotions
Define actions required	Break a promise
Be brief and to the point	Be late

SOCIABLE:

DO	DON'T
Be energetic/enthusiastic	Be negative
Make it fun	Get into long conversations
Be inspirational	Bore them with excess detail
Tap into their ideas	Be too formal

CARING:

DO	DON'T
Be sensitive and supportive	Be aggressive
Use a quiet tone of voice	Be impersonal and formal
Ask meaningful questions	Be too direct
Listen and show an interest	Rush them

DETAILED:

DO	DON'T
Plan and prepare	Rush them
Go into detail	Be pushy
Be on time	Be over friendly
Be logical and formal	Be flippant or fast paced

Over twenty-five years of delivering successful training sessions, I have found the key element is *how* I deliver the skills. Every audience is different, and it's essential I adapt my communication style in order to connect with the delegates in front of me.

For example, I have a client based in Basel, Switzerland. The delegates I train for this client are highly intelligent, thoughtful, fairly serious Swiss nationals with a financial/accountancy background – a room full of Detailed types. When running leadership training events there, I adapt my instinctive style/behaviour by toning down my usual upbeat, enthusiastic approach. I am much more correct, more formal, more serious for the day.

I have another client in New York where I run sales training programmes. Here the room is crammed full of Sociable types who are upbeat, loud and chatty. With them, I am energetic, animated, enthusiastic and fast-paced in my approach.

A third example is a UK client that provides care homes and walk-in surgeries for the elderly. I run a series of management training courses for Team Leaders who are the Caring type – predominately considerate, kind and patient. Here I adapt my behaviour to be more approachable, supportive and amenable.

With all three examples, I don't alter or change my *personality*; I adapt my *behaviour*.

OVER TO YOU

Think of someone at work with whom you would like to have a better relationship. What do you think is *their* preferred personality type (Direct, Sociable, Caring or Detailed)?

What small adaptation should *you* make next time you are in front of them?

THE VALUE OF ADAPTING

My wife Helen and I recently celebrated our tenth wedding anniversary with a special weekend treat at a beautiful luxury country hotel. When we'd parked outside the entrance, we were greeted at reception by a warm welcome from Kate.

Having checked us in, Kate said, 'Mr Saunders, if you give me your car keys, I'll get Frank to park your car and take your luggage directly to your room.'

Now, maybe this is just me, but I was thinking, woah there, I don't really let strangers into my car, and all my stuff is in there, and who is this Frank anyway?

Kate looked at me, read my mind, and with a lovely smile said gently, 'Just let go.'

Brilliant. She'd worked me out in a second and said exactly the right thing, causing both Helen and I to laugh out loud. I handed over the keys like an obedient child.

But then Kate demonstrated her real talent – the ability to adapt her communication style effortlessly. She chatted to Helen in a friendly manner, talking about the hotel's spa treatments and the spectacular afternoon tea, so within seconds, Helen was also putty in her hands.

And as we were standing there talking, another guest

approached reception. He looked serious, earnest, a little stressed. Kate took on a different approach with him – less jovial and more formal. She answered his questions politely, professionally, in just the right manner, making him feel special. We could tell he was impressed.

We had a great weekend at the hotel. Would we go back? Sure.

However, the question is not would we go back there, but why?

And the answer is not Kate; the answer is how she made us feel. The impact she had on Helen and I by making us feel relaxed, comfortable and welcome was all achieved by her adapting her style of communication.

THE COST OF NOT ADAPTING

Once upon a time, there was a young engineer. He worked in an enclosed office cubicle, designing personal computers and scientific calculators. An introvert, he liked to work alone, preferring solitude over committees and team meetings.

His name was Steve Wozniak. And he invented the first Apple computer.

But because he was an introvert and kept himself

to himself, Wozniak's managers at Hewlett-Packard didn't recognise the magnitude of what he'd created. He didn't fit the HP mould of being outgoing and visible, and in turn, they didn't adapt to the way he did things. They stuck to their inflexible methods and turned down his prototype five times before he left to form a business relationship with Steve Jobs.

If the leaders at HP had adapted to Wozniak's style and way of working, they wouldn't have lost the pioneer of the personal computer revolution... or billions of dollars.

BACK TO DAD

So there I was with Dad, talking about adapting, and suddenly, just to stress the point, he adapted his commination style with me – right there.

He looked serious and boomed, 'When I say adapt, that doesn't mean lie!'

He continued, 'Don't be dishonest. Adapting your style is not about being false or disingenuous. This is not about changing your personality.

'How you behave with someone is a choice. A small adaptation to your behaviour means you can rub along with them better to reach a mutually beneficial outcome.'

Dad was adamant about this.

'You *must* tell the truth. Patients came to see me to find out what was medically wrong with them. So the conversations were sometimes difficult, but it was never my job to mislead them in any way.'

To collaborate with people better, we all need to adapt our style accordingly. I don't mean change who we are or how we normally talk, but a 5% shift in our behaviour so we are more in tune with the person in front of us works like magic.

Here is an email I received from a client (a Relationship Manager at a bank) that sums up the power of adapting.

Hi Nick,

My name is David and I was at your session last week which I thoroughly enjoyed, particularly the part about adapting your style when in front of someone. I know I am fairly laid back and sometimes too gentle with clients. I have one client in particular who is very direct. I've been trying to finalise a deal with him for over six months and he has been aggressive and abrupt in wanting the transaction to be done his particular way.

In a meeting with him yesterday, I heeded your advice and adapted my style to being more assertive and upfront with him, talking about the realities of how the deal should be structured (I didn't find this easy, by the way). Initially, the client looked a little shocked, but twenty minutes later, you'll be delighted to know he agreed to sign the deal.

It's a £25million transaction that has earnt us
£2million net. Just thought you'd like to know.

Regards,

David.

Two observations here: 1 – that's the power of adapting;
2 – what a mug I was for not agreeing commission up front.

RECAP
ADAPT

1. Adapt your language, tone, style

2. Which personality type is the person in
front of you?

3. Apply the Dos and Don'ts for each type

4. This is not about changing personality;
it's about adapting behaviour.

CHAPTER 6
BE AUTHENTIC

"I had no idea that being your authentic self could make me as rich as I've become. If I had, I'd have done it a lot earlier."

—

Oprah Winfrey

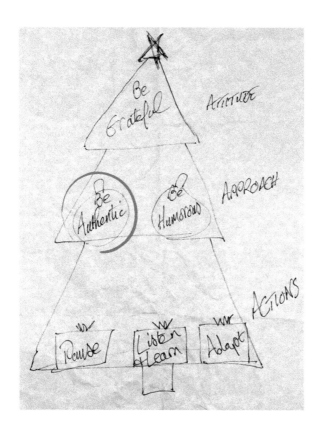

Mr Authentic

By now, Dad was on his fourth glass of wine and on a roll.

'OK, Nick. A quick recap of the three actions. First, pause to stop your natural, emotional response. Then, be curious. Listen and learn about the person in front of you. Finally, adapt your approach to give them what they need.'

Dad then went back to his diagram of the tree, and on the right-hand side in the middle, wrote the word 'Approach'.

'There are two approaches you need to adopt. The first is to be authentic.'

Now what does authentic really mean? The dictionary definition is: *not false or copied; genuine; real.* My personal definition is: *just be you.*

And who do we think of as truly authentic? Nelson Mandela, Lord Alan Sugar, Ant and Dec, Jeremy Corbyn?

Some people I've asked have mentioned Richard Branson as someone who is authentic. By his own admission, he's a shy man and not necessarily the world's best communicator in certain situations. When being interviewed or presenting, he's often ill at ease, sometimes looks nervous, and fumbles incessantly. This could be seen as a weakness, but actually, it's Richard Branson. That's just the man he is.

When Branson was starting out in business and trying to launch the Virgin brand, he was in dire need of significant finance. He and his business partner, Nick Powell, had a meeting at a bank to try and secure a substantial loan. Powell turned up for the meeting in a smart suit and tie; Branson turned up in ripped jeans and a scruffy white shirt.

Powell said to Branson, 'What on earth are you wearing?'

Branson replied, 'Don't worry about what I'm wearing. What are you wearing? You look like a smartly dressed heroin addict about to be sentenced in court. I look like someone who doesn't care enough to need the money.'

Branson dressed his way; he was being his authentic self. And yes, they got the loan.

GAINING TRUST THROUGH AUTHENTICITY

Building relationships is all about trust – and trust comes from authenticity. It's important to say and do the things you actually believe because that's what people look for. If you're not authentic or put out false messages, you lose people's trust.

Trust is about understanding and opening up to one another, but not in a touchy-feely kind of way. In fact, there is nothing touchy-feely about it at all. Earning trust is about not holding back; not being afraid to air mistakes; not being afraid to show weaknesses and concerns.

And trust is a two-way thing. Human beings have a deeply-rooted tendency towards reciprocity. We are naturally inclined to want to help, do favours for, reward people who have done these things for us first.

And the same holds true when it comes to trust. We are more likely to feel we can trust someone who has trusted us first.

TRUST IN BUSINESS

Those who live in blind trust will almost certainly get burned. Those who trust no one will eventually experience some kind of financial, social or emotional loss. Successful companies and people find a middle way called 'smart trust'.

For example, eBay has hundreds of millions of registered users, nearly all of whom are complete strangers to each other. Yet they engage in over one million financial transactions a day.

Former eBay CEO Meg Whitman says, 'I still believe the fundamental reason eBay works is that people everywhere are basically good.'

Netflix built a thriving film rental business based on trust. Initially, it trusted all its customers to send back their DVDs, occasionally eliminating unreliable customers as a cost of doing business. If Netflix hadn't extended this original trust, it wouldn't have nearly as many subscribers today.

Gerry Spence is an outstanding American trial lawyer who has practised law since the 1960s. From 1960 to 2017, Spence has never lost a criminal case – either as a prosecutor or a defence attorney. He says the secret to winning an argument or influencing someone is to get people to trust you – and in order to get people to trust you, you have to find something about their point that you authentically agree with.

BEING AUTHENTIC – WITH TECHNIQUE

So I agree it's important to be authentic, to be you, to be genuine. However, the key is to be authentic *with technique*. Be you, but use skills to enhance your goals.

Professor Herminia Ibarra is a world renowned and respected

economist who specialises in leadership. She wrote an article in The *Harvard Business Review* called 'The Authenticity Paradox' which focuses on how authenticity has become the gold standard for leadership. But she points out the importance of being flexible and having the ability to adapt our behaviour where appropriate.

> *Be true to yourself. But which self? We have many selves depending on the different roles we have in life. I say what I feel. Fine, but there will be times when you will lose credibility and effectiveness (as a leader) if you disclose everything you think and feel.*

— Professor Herminia Ibarra

AN AUTHENTIC CONVERSATION

Here is a simple four point plan I teach that can be used when you need to have an authentic, honest conversation with someone to gain their respect/trust and achieve a mutually beneficial outcome.

The issue
Be concise and get to the point straight away.

Why it's important
Explain what's at stake, the significance, the consequence if it's not resolved.

What I want – my ideal outcome
State the perfect result from your point of view.

How we all win
Illustrate the benefits of your idea/proposal to the other person, you and the team/organisation.

This four point plan can be used in a variety of situations, e.g. delegating a task, issuing instructions, giving feedback. Here is an example of using the four point plan for a difficult conversation with a colleague about their recent behaviour.

The issue:
'Dave, I've got an important issue that I want to discuss with you. It's about the way you sometimes talk over me, cut me off mid-sentence and dismiss my ideas. This has happened on a couple of occasions, most recently at the last team meeting.'

Why it's important:
'This is quite serious and there is a great deal at stake here. When you behave like this, it impacts me, the team and other colleagues. It also affects my work and our relationship.'

What I want – my ideal outcome:
'What I'd really like is for you to take responsibility and change the way you sometimes communicate. This will help prevent inappropriate behaviour ruining our working partnership.'

How we all win:
'If you do this, I'm sure there will be a significant difference in how we get on. You'll find it much easier to win me and

others over *and* you'll get your projects finished on time without excess stress. This can only have a positive impact and help deliver the results we are all aiming to achieve.'

OVER TO YOU

Think of a conversation you've had in the past, or even better, a conversation coming up that may be challenging where you want to be assertive and authentic. Use the four step plan to jot down some thoughts on how you might tackle it.

The issue:

Why it's important:

What I want – my ideal outcome:

How we all win:

THE AUTHENTIC LEADER

Some leaders may feel pressure to change their personality to match their role. The problem is if they start to be false or insincere, those around them will soon suss this out and feel they're being deceived. Then the leader is surprised to hear they're not liked, trusted, respected – and even more surprised when people leave the organisation.

Individuals at work need to be influenced by someone who is genuine, communicates in a compelling way and can excel at capturing people's hearts, minds and souls. If leaders remain authentic, they will be more effective, productive and inspiring. Authentic leadership requires the leader to bring their whole self to work.

BEING *TOO* AUTHENTIC AND HONEST

But here's a counter-intuitive truth: being honest about *everything* all the time is not the panacea it's sometimes painted as. Many people at some point have been truly authentic and honest and said it like it is, only to produce a less than desirable outcome.

I clearly remember one of my old bosses asking me for honest feedback on a business presentation he'd made to a client. So, I was authentic and honest, while being diplomatic and careful with my words. I remarked that in my opinion, the presentation was a little longwinded, and at certain points, the audience looked confused. My boss took my comments well – apart from throwing his phone against a wall and not speaking to me for a week.

I'm not advocating that it's bad to be honest. I'm not saying we should never tell it how it is. However, to be great influencers, leaders and managers, we need to control our emotions and adapt our behaviour in order to reach the right outcome. We need the skill of being authentic while being accommodating, tempering our true feelings and controlling our impulses. In other words, we need to say the right things at the right time to the right people.

Sometimes we need to be careful not to damage a relationship. Sometimes, if the emotion takes over and we're truly authentic, saying what we think at an instinctive, raw, heartfelt level, it can have ramifications.

Gerald Ratner was being truly authentic when he described his jewellery as 'total crap', a comment that instantly wiped £500 million from the value of his business.

John Pluthero, UK Chairman of Cable & Wireless, sent a memo to the whole organisation:

Congratulations! We work for an underperforming business in a crappy industry and it's going to be hell for the next 12 months. If you are worried that it all sounds very hard, it's time for you to step off the bus.

There is an amusing Ricky Gervais film called *The Invention of Lying* in which no one lies. Gervais's character is at a restaurant on a dinner date with a beautiful woman. Her mobile rings, and she has a conversation right in front of him.

'Hi, Mum. Yes, I'm with him right now. No, not very attractive, doesn't make much money. Seems nice but a bit fat, has a funny little snub nose. No, I won't be sleeping with him. No, not even a kiss.'

CHAMPIONS OF AUTHENTIC LEADERSHIP

Bill George from Harvard Business School conducted a study into authentic leadership, asking readers for their vote on the most authentic leader. One respondent nominated Warren Buffett, the American business magnate and philanthropist who is considered to be one of the most successful investors in the world.

My choice would be Warren Buffett. Warren displays authentic leadership in showing a real commitment both in words and deeds to improving 'stakeholder value' over time. By stakeholders, I mean shareholders, employees, customers, the community, etc. Warren is both a great leader and a great teacher. He is an independent thinker who challenges the conventionally accepted way of looking at things, and explains his reasoning in a sound and uncomplicated way.

Another respondent nominated Ratan Tata of the Tata Group, a highly successful Indian businessman, investor and philanthropist.

Chairman Ratan Tata is the epitome of authentic leadership because he has the ability to bring the Globe to India and take India to the Globe. He lives the Tata life and is a model of inspiration for young managers within the Tata Group. It takes the best leadership aptitude and intuition to hold a group consisting of ninety-eight worldwide companies together successfully in a unique network, and Chairman Tata achieves this on a daily basis.

RECAP
BE AUTHENTIC

1. People are drawn to individuals who truly *are* what they seem to be

2. Authenticity is the foundation to earning respect

3. Mean what you say and say what you mean

4. Be authentic while being accommodating

5. Convey you have clear principles and act on them

6. Show you are reliable and can be depended upon.

CHAPTER 7
BE HUMOROUS

"To make mistakes is human; to
stumble is commonplace; to be able to
laugh at yourself is maturity."

—

William Arthur Ward, author

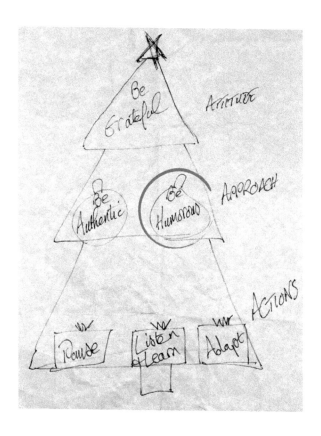

Dad's next principle to getting on with anyone surprised me a little – be humorous about yourself. This means laughing at yourself, not taking yourself too seriously, self-deprecation.

When people laugh at themselves, they show their human side. They are comfortable revealing selective weaknesses such as an interpersonal shortcoming or a mistake they've made in the past. It is only when individuals are comfortable exposing these weaknesses to one another that they can act without concern for protecting themselves. They reveal a vulnerability which, in turn, establishes trust, solidarity and empathy.

A lovable, self-deprecating show-off

The CEO of a large business came up to me after a talk recently. He remarked that he liked the principle of self-deprecation and that my dad was obviously a funny man, but he could never be like that.

I explained that being humorous isn't about being like my dad. Being humorous in this context does not mean suddenly turning into a comedian. It's about being able to laugh at yourself at the appropriate time and in the appropriate place.

WARNING!

Laughing at yourself must be done carefully. It is important not to expose a weakness that may be seen as a fatal flaw. As a respected surgeon, if Dad had admitted he didn't know where the liver or kidney was, it wouldn't have been funny. A Finance Director at a large corporation suddenly confessing he's never understood discounted cash flow would not be a good move.

Too much self-deprecating humour may backfire, or come across as insincere and fake.

THE POWER OF SELF-DEPRECATION

But self-deprecation can be extremely beneficial, even in the sometimes stiff, serious corporate world. A recent study found that leaders who can laugh at themselves (rather than at their colleagues or direct reports) are seen as more likable, trustworthy, and caring.

Researchers Colette Hoption, Julian Barling and Nick Turner (Seattle University) discovered that, regardless of whether people actually thought a leader was funny, they saw self-deprecating jokes as an expression of a leader's values.

> *Leaders who focus on self-deprecation and the*
> *well-being of others are more likely to earn the*
> *trust and good will of their employees. Poking fun*
> *at themselves may be one way in which leaders*
> *can de-emphasise differences in status between*
> *themselves and their employees, providing*
> *evidence of their concern for others.*
>
> — Hoption, Barling and Turner

The researchers conducted an exercise where a group of undergraduates were presented with three scenarios in which a company MD introduced a new team member, Paul. The three scenarios were exactly the same, until it came to the punchline.

The first scenario ended with the boss saying, 'I'm delighted Paul has taken the job, despite knowing all about us!'

The second scenario ended with: 'I'm delighted Paul has taken the job, despite knowing all about you lot!'

The third scenario ended with: 'I'm delighted Paul has taken the job, despite knowing all about me!'

Almost unanimously, the undergraduates rated the boss in the third scenario – the self-deprecating boss – as the most likeable and trustworthy.

WHY CORPORATE SELF-DEPRECATION WORKS

Many companies use self-deprecation as a deliberate advertising strategy to sell more products.

> *Presenting yourself as perfect is not as persuasive as some people think it is. Admitting your perceived weakness is a pretty effective strategy. It inspires trust.*

— Rory Sutherland, Vice Chairman of the advertising agency, Ogilvy Group UK

Volkswagen's 'Think Small and Lemon' advert in 1959 was unusual in drawing attention to the VW Beetle's perceived weaknesses. Now it is seen as one of the best advertisements ever conceived.

Private Eye nicknamed *The Guardian* newspaper *The Grauniad* after its legendary spelling mistakes. Now the paper has gone as far as to use Grauniad.co.uk as a redirect to its homepage.

Marks & Spencer launched the famous ad campaign 'We Boobed' following an outcry over its charging policy for bras.

Skoda, once the butt of many a joke, used the successful strapline 'It's a Skoda. Honest'.

Even countries use self-deprecating humour. The 2014 Sochi Winter Olympic Games closed with Russia poking fun at itself. In the opening ceremony, a lighting malfunction led to one of the Olympic rings remaining closed, and this malfunction dominated coverage. However, demonstrating that the Russians do have a sense of humour, hundreds of dancers in the closing ceremony formed the Olympic rings – with the fifth ring of dancers initially failing to open.

KEEP YOUR EGO IN CHECK

Of course, there are some leaders and managers who have no desire to demonstrate self-deprecation. Many of them display behaviours driven by ego, pride, self-importance and arrogance.

Over-inflated egos tend to lead to conversations turning into lectures, team meetings into sermons, discussions into monologues. With ego comes a loss of trust and respect.

People won't want to work with these leaders, let alone collaborate with them.

In the bestselling book *Why CEOs Fail*, the authors Dotlich and Cairo list the common behaviours that cause CEOs to fail, including:

- Arrogance
- Disrespecting colleagues
- Dismissing ideas
- Purporting to be more knowledgeable than others
- Avoiding blame
- Pinning blame on others
- Discounting feedback.

History demonstrates this. Enron's CEO Jeff Skilling had a huge ego. His confidence in Enron's innovations in trading natural gas and electricity impressed financial analysts. But ultimately, his arrogance led to Enron's bankruptcy, and he is currently serving a prison sentence having been indicted on thirty-five counts of fraud, insider trading and other crimes related to the scandal.

In 2008, Thor Bjorgolfsson became the biggest investor in Iceland's banks. When he went to bed on Friday 3 October 2008, he was worth £3 billion. By Monday night, he'd lost the lot! Several banks, and the country itself, went bust.

In forty-eight hours, he became the Fred Goodwin (the disgraced former boss of RBS) of Iceland.

Bjorgolfsson was blamed for borrowing too much to buy Landsbanki and driving it and the banking system over a cliff. Why did he do it?

> *Ambition and ego. I was driven by personal competitiveness and rivalry. I wanted to outdo my peers.*

> — Thor Bjorgolfsson

TIPS ON SELF-DEPRECATION

Peter McGraw, Marketing and Psychology Professor at the University of Colorado, Boulder, wrote *The Humor Code*. In his book, he lists recommendations and tips on how to be more self-deprecating:

> *It's not whether you're funny, it's what kind of funny you are. Be honest and authentic. If you can't be 'ha-ha' funny, be 'aha!' funny. Cleverness is often good enough. Chuckle at yourself. It signals everything is OK. Laughter is disarming. Poke fun at the stuff everyone's worried about.*

> *One more useful tip – to tell whether a colleague's amusement is real (rather than fake), look for crinkling around the eyes. If it's there, you've got true 'Duchenne' laughter (named after the French physician who identified it).*

At the 2010 White House Correspondents' Dinner, Barack Obama mocked his own declining popularity.

> *It's been quite a year since I've spoken here last – lots of ups, lots of downs – except for my approval ratings, which have just gone down. It doesn't bother me. Besides, I happen to know that my approval ratings are still very high in the country of my birth.*

I worked with a well-known ferry company that was looking to raise significant investment in its business. It had secured a meeting with a capital venture firm in the City, and the Board asked me to help put together a pitch to secure the funds.

We spent many hours preparing the presentation. Come the day, each Board member stood up and spoke about their part of the business. Half way through the presentation, we had a break and the CEO pulled me to one side and asked how I thought it was all going.

Although there had been much focus on figures and income, I felt strongly that the investors needed to buy into the culture of the company. There was a lack of connection and empathy between those presenting and the audience. I suggested to the CEO, a jovial and witty man, that when it was his turn to speak, he should add a touch of self-deprecating humour and lightness to win over the room.

Needless to say, he did just that and was superb. He regaled the group with twenty minutes of self-deprecating stories, reflecting on his own management style. The whole atmosphere changed. And yes, they secured the funds.

OVER TO YOU

List three of your faults/weaknesses.

1

2

3

Jot down a self-deprecating story about something that's happened to you that you'd be prepared to share where appropriate.

RECAP
BE HUMOROUS

1. Laugh at yourself – don't take yourself too seriously

2. Revealing a vulnerability establishes trust, solidarity and empathy

3. Don't expose a weakness that will be seen as a fatal flaw

4. Self-deprecation shows our human side – we're not perfect!

CHAPTER 8
BE GRATEFUL

"As we express our gratitude, we must never forget that the highest appreciation is not to utter words, but to live by them."

—

John F. Kennedy

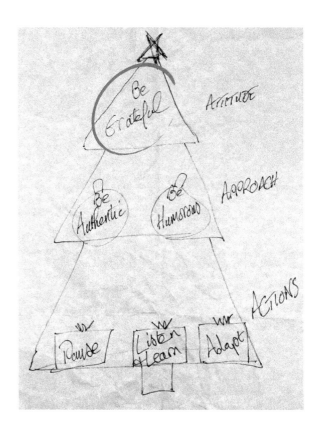

The night was drawing in. Dad and I had been talking for hours and it was obvious he was tired. As he referred back to his drawing of the tree, I could see his hand was shaking. It was difficult seeing someone who had always been so physically fit look so frail, but I felt very close to him as we sat chatting together for what turned out to be one of the last times.

Dad took the pen and wrote *Attitude* at the top of the tree. Next to this, he wrote two words: *be grateful*.

He said, 'Nick, be grateful for everything you have.'

Initially, I was a bit sceptical. I remember thinking at the time, *Isn't that a little corny? Be grateful?* But Dad wasn't in any way a cheesy, shallow guy. He didn't go around telling people to be grateful. In fact, I don't think it was something I'd ever heard him say before. As outgoing as he was, he was still very British. And this wasn't the kind of conversation most British fathers had with their sons. I think he knew the end was coming and was feeling a little emotional as he looked back on his life.

But I soon got it. If you want to get people on your side, be grateful. Show gratitude. People are drawn to those who are thankful for the work they do and the effort they make.

My dad spent his life thanking people and showing his appreciation. I remember spending a day in theatre at his hospital, watching several operations. Dad was one of five surgeons who performed operations that day, and when it was his case, all the theatre staff's attitudes changed. The whole atmosphere became positive and upbeat. And he was the only doctor that day to thank the staff.

NO REGRETS

In simple terms, I think there is a link between having an attitude of gratitude and having no regrets. If you don't show gratitude throughout your life, you may regret it later.

There is a thought-provoking, powerful book written by palliative care nurse Bronnie Ware called *The Top Five Regrets of the Dying*. This remarkable woman spent her life caring for those who had only days or weeks left to live. As she nursed her patients and they got to know her, they would open up and reveal regrets as they looked back on their lives. Bronnie Ware knew the people who would benefit most from this list were the living, so she wrote a book listing the five most common regrets.

They are:

- **I wish I'd had the courage to live a life true to myself**
- **I wish I hadn't worked so hard**
- **I wish I'd had the courage to express my feelings**

- I wish I had stayed in touch with my friends
- I wish I had let myself be happier.

The interesting thing about Dad is that he didn't have any regrets – simply because he had been grateful, lived his life true to himself, been authentic, humorous, kept in touch with all his friends. And I had such enormous respect for him for that.

And I guess I realised at that moment what he meant by 'be grateful'. He was a naturally grateful man. It was his attitude of gratitude that created his gregarious, generous, kind, thoughtful, empathic and extraordinarily self-controlled mindset.

Arnold Bennett, the British novelist, had a publisher who boasted about the extraordinary efficiency of his PA. One day, while visiting the publisher's office, Bennett said, 'Your boss claims you're extremely efficient. What's your secret?'

'It's not my secret,' said the PA. 'It's his. Each time I do something for him, no matter how insignificant, he never fails to appreciate it and show his gratitude.'

Because of this, she took infinite pains with her work and remained a loyal employee for over thirty years.

THE BENEFITS OF BEING GRATEFUL AT WORK

Being grateful isn't just about the softer side of collaboration. There is evidence demonstrating how being grateful in the workplace reaps many benefits – tangible, measurable business benefits.

Gratitude increases motivation

Studies show gratitude promotes significant increases in determination, attention, enthusiasm and energy. According to Globoforce's Spring 2014 Workforce Mood Tracker survey, 86% of employees who were recognised at work felt more motivated in their jobs. The survey pointed out that managers who remembered to say thank you to people working for them found those employees worked harder.

Researchers at the University of Pennsylvania randomly divided university fundraisers into two groups. One group made phone calls to solicit donations in the same way they always had. The second group received a pep talk from the Director of Annual Giving, who told the fundraisers she was grateful for their efforts. During the following week, the employees who'd heard her message of gratitude made 50% more fundraising calls than those who had not.

Gratitude increases a sense of commitment

Professor Adam Grant studied a Fortune 500 company that allowed employees to contribute to an employee beneficiary fund. He found donors rather than beneficiaries had the greater increase in affective commitment to the company.

Additionally, Globoforce's Spring 2012 Workforce Mood Tracker study found 80% of those who felt appreciated at work wanted to stay at the company, as opposed to 60% who did not feel appreciated and were job searching.

Gratitude increases engagement

The 2013 Workforce Mood Tracker study found that employees who had been empowered to give recognition to peers were more than twice as engaged as those who had not. The impact of engagement on ROI is enormous: research from Towers Watson shows that engaged employees are more productive and more profitable.

In an article from *Harvard Business Review*, a study by Adam Grant and Francesca Gino shows how ingratitude – not being acknowledged or thanked – means people very quickly stop wanting to help. When someone isn't thanked for their help, their future rates of helping people drop by 50%.

THE SECRET OF SUCCESS – BE POSITIVE

Psychologist Shawn Achor is the CEO of Goodthink Inc. The company researches and teaches about positive psychology. He says that if our brains are at a positive setting, they perform significantly better than brains at a negative or stressed setting. Our intelligence, creativity and energy rise.

His research shows a positive outlook is one of the greatest competitive advantages in the modern economy, with vast improvement in business outcomes: 31% higher productivity, 37% higher sales, three times greater creativity and 23% fewer fatigue symptoms. Happy people are also up to ten times more engaged, 40% more likely to receive a promotion and 39% more likely to live to ninety-four.

Have a look at Shawn Achor's excellent speech on TED Talks – 'The happy secret to better work'.

www.ted.com/talks/shawn_achor_the_happy_secret_to_ better_work

Yet unfortunately, our brains are trained to spot the negatives. We tend to focus on mistakes, failures and criticism, which weakens our ability to process and see the positive. Achor says the good news is we can re-train our brains.

With practice and repetition, we can re-programme ourselves to change how we filter, interpret and react to the world. By actively finding ways to practise gratitude, joy and social connection, we encourage our brains to retain a pattern of scanning the world for the positive rather than the negative.

HOW TO BUILD A CULTURE OF GRATITUDE

It has to start with the boss like any culture change at any organisation. If you are going to encourage a genuine attitude of gratitude in your business, employees first need to hear 'Thank you' from the bosses, those with the power, consistently and authentically in both public and private settings.

Everyone should be thanked. It's easy to thank those in high-profile positions or those who do the 'important' stuff. But thanking those who do the less visible and less glamorous work is crucial because it establishes the right tone throughout the organisation. Public appreciation of those who are easily forgotten can only improve morale and increase trust.

Be genuine. Praising for praise's sake, insincere or 'over the top' praise doesn't work. It undermines gratitude and will make genuine expressions of gratitude feel inauthentic. People can always tell when you are being insincere, and your compliment will backfire. And too much gratitude induces gratitude fatigue.

The key is to encourage opportunities that foster voluntary, spontaneous expressions of gratitude.

Be specific. A generic over-used 'I appreciate your hard work' doesn't cut it. People will feel you're just saying it for the sake of saying it, or you'll come across as someone who wants to say thank you, but you don't actually know what you're thanking them for.

Be unexpected. It's common to express gratitude at the end of a job, project, the financial year, or just as you set off on holiday. But it can feel as though you are going through the motions and ticking off points on your gratitude to-do list. Spontaneous thanks mean more because people know you didn't have to thank them, or even notice their hard work, but you did.

SHOWING GRATITUDE IN THE RIGHT WAY

The key is to give praise in the right way: a quiet word in private; an email copying in the whole organisation; a handwritten thank-you note; keeping a praise journal; having an appreciation platform webpage; creating a bulletin board for praise; giving a gift; handing out coffee and cake; taking the whole company to the Bahamas for a week.

The simple act of showing gratitude can lead to more trust in working relationships if it's reciprocal, sincere, and altruistically motivated.

HOW TO GIVE EFFECTIVE PRAISE

Praising people encourages them to do well. Most people, however accomplished and apparently confident, experience praise deprivation from time to time.

It is common that when things go well, nothing gets said, but when things go badly, it is certainly noticed. Giving effective praise is a simple yet powerful skill – the two Ws technique. When you're praising someone, start by explaining specifically *what* they did right. Then tell them *why* it was good in terms of outcome, results or consequences.

For example:

What: 'That was an excellent presentation, Steve. What I really enjoyed was your use of anecdotes and personal stories.'

Why: 'This brought the theoretical part of the presentation to life, and you could see the audience got the message. Well done!'

OVER TO YOU

Think of a time in the past when a colleague did something deserving of genuine praise. Or even better, is there someone who deserves to be praised today? Jot down some words.

What:

Why:

MEANINGFUL THANKS

Business psychiatrist, Mark Goulston, wrote an interesting article about giving meaningful thanks in the Harvard Business Review.

In my line of work, I frequently communicate with CEOs and their executive assistants, and nowhere is the need for gratitude more clear.

After one CEO's assistant had been particularly helpful, I replied to her email with a grateful, "I hope your company and your boss know and let you know how valuable and special you are."

She emailed back, "You don't know how much your email meant to me." It made me wonder — when was the last time her boss had thanked her?

This happens frequently. For instance, a few years ago, I was trying to get in touch with one of the world's most well-known CEOs about an article. His assistant had done a great and friendly job of gatekeeping. So when I wrote to her boss, I included this: "When I get to be rich, I'm going to hire someone like your assistant — to protect me from people like me. She was helpful, friendly, feisty vs. boring and yet guarded access to you like a loyal pit bull. If she doesn't know how valuable she is to you, you are making a big managerial mistake and YOU should know better."

A week later I called his assistant, and said, "I don't know if you remember me, but I'm just following up on a letter and article I sent to your boss to see if he received it."

His assistant replied warmly, 'Of course I remember you, Dr. Mark. About your letter and article. I sent him the article, but not your cover letter.'

I thought, 'Uh, oh! I messed up.' Haltingly, I asked why.

She responded with the delight of someone who had just served an ace in a tennis match: 'I didn't send it to him, I read it to him over the phone.'

Needless to say, that assistant and I have remained friends ever since.

AN ATTITUDE OF GRATITUDE

My grandfather, Dr John Watts, was a remarkable man. He served as a surgeon in the Army and, during a long and distinguished career, saved literally hundreds of lives in campaigns all over the world. He was awarded the OBE for services to his country.

He was also a shining example of how to live a life with an attitude of gratitude.

Aged eighty and happily retired, he and his wife lived a tranquil life in Suffolk. One day, they went on a shopping trip to an outdoor gardening centre. When they'd finished buying what they needed, my grandmother went to get the car (a large Volvo estate) while my grandfather waited with a young shop assistant.

As Gran drove around to the front of the centre, she unfortunately pressed down on the accelerator instead of the brake. Consequently, she drove into my grandfather and the young man, who flew backwards into the large plate-glass window severing two major arteries in his leg. Gran carried on accelerating in a full circle and came round again – this time running over her husband, shattering his pelvis, liver and bladder in the process. Undaunted, Gran kept going and hit a parked car which shot backwards, knocking over a woman.

Eventually, she stopped.

Two ambulances arrived, and the crew understandably went straight to the screaming young man lying in a pool of blood, initially leaving my grandfather, who looked less distressed. When they finally turned their attention to my grandfather, they checked his vital signs and decided he was not badly injured, unaware that he had suffered major internal injuries and was quietly bleeding to death. They eventually got him to hospital where, fortunately, a sharp-eyed doctor noticed he was in trouble and instructed the trauma team to get him into surgery immediately.

Thankfully, he survived (as did the young shop assistant who made a full recovery), but my grandfather endured a long stint recovering in hospital.

Gran was mortified at what she'd done, and visited him every day. On one visit, she went to sit down, missed the chair and broke her leg in three places.

At least they could recover together.

My grandfather spent ten months in hospital, was confined to a wheelchair for a year and spent the rest of his life in pain and discomfort. Not once did he complain. Not once did he moan or whinge. He had always said how grateful he was for the life he'd led. Even after the accident, his attitude of gratitude never changed.

My grandfather – clever, funny and grateful

THE POWER OF THANK YOU

I've been working with my local garage, giving some business advice to the friendly and helpful owners, Paul and Gavin. Although the garage is well established and successful, they wanted to increase turnover – so we came up with the simple idea of giving every customer a personalised thank you note.

Each customer finds the following letter (along with a chocolate) in their car when they pick it up.

We just wanted to say a big thank you for giving us the chance to work on your car. We are very aware that as a customer, you have the choice on deciding which garage to use. We genuinely appreciate your business and trust you will be satisfied with the work we have done.

Anytime you need us, or rather your car needs us, just call.

Best wishes,

Paul and Gavin.

The feedback from customers has been excellent – they love the note and tell others about it, resulting in an 18% increase in bookings.

OVER TO YOU

If you had only months to live...

Who would you thank?

What would you say?

What's stopping you?

RECAP
BE GRATEFUL

1. Be grateful for everything you have

2. Praise more often – at home and at work

3. Develop an 'attitude of gratitude'

4. Have no regrets.

CHAPTER 9
TO SUM UP

"You can choose your friends but you sho'
can't choose your family,"

—

Harper Lee

The chances are that you didn't get to choose your family, neither the one at home nor the one at work. And there will be some members of both families who will, at times, drive you crazy. If not, great. You're cured!

But here's the thing – you have a choice. Either you can let them continue to drive you mad with frustration or you can develop some sort of strategy for getting on with them more effectively on a day-to-day basis. And here is your strategy.

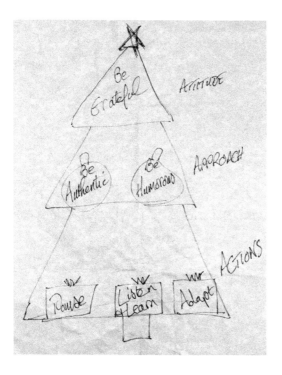

I don't pretend it's the definitive 'there-is-no-better-way' model. However, broadly speaking, it works. I say 'broadly speaking' because I don't know *anyone*, in either business or everyday life, who manages to put this model into practice every moment of every day.

It's Dad's model, and he was remarkable with people, but he wasn't perfect. He used to get frustrated – of course he did. At some point in our lives, we've all lost it; acted inappropriately; said something we later regret. Using the six skills isn't always easy and we're not going to be able to use them in *every* situation – because we're human.

But they do work.

When I go into businesses and organisations to teach these principles, and people embrace and use them, the results are always the same: less disagreements, less bickering and less confrontation. And better teamwork, better cooperation, better collaboration... all of which ultimately lead to better performance. These principles turn relationships into results.

At home with Luke and Helen, I make a real effort to use the skills. I don't always manage it, but I make a genuine attempt to pause, especially when stressed. I want to know about their day, their thoughts, their view of things. I adapt my style while being authentic, don't take myself seriously, and above all, I'm grateful to have a wonderful wife and son.

The aim of this book is to give you simple, practical skills that can have a huge impact, not to change, alter or transform you into something you're not. It is about making small adaptations to your behaviour when the situation demands it.

IT'S THE SMALL THINGS

And when I say small, I mean small. A 5% shift in how you behave with people can make a massive difference. This shift when using the six principles can radically improve a conversation.

Sir Clive Woodward, the rugby union coach who guided England to victory in the 2003 Rugby World Cup, attributes much of that success to 'the critical non-essentials'. He wanted his players to do 'a hundred things just 1% better'.

Formula 1's McLaren team talks about 'tenths'. The whole organisation is besotted by the idea of shaving tenths of a second off the lap time.

John Wooden of UCLA Bruins basketball team won the US national championship seven years on the trot. He is revered as one of the great American sporting leaders – because he focused on the small things. For example, he got his teams to spend hours learning how to put on their socks!

*Check the heel area. We don't want any sign of a
wrinkle about it ... The wrinkle will be sure you
get blisters, and those blisters are going to make
you lose playing time, and if you're good enough,
your loss of playing time might get the coach fired.*

BJ Fogg at Stanford University is known for his research
called 'Tiny Habits'. This works on the premise that you
start doing something small and it becomes a habit.

The idea is you make a clear statement of the new behaviour
you want. State the cue, the thought that will remind you to
undertake the new behaviour, and then actually do it. The
trick is to make the new behaviour really tiny.

The great Muhammad Ali said, 'It isn't the mountains ahead
to climb that wear you out; it's the pebble in your shoe.'

Last Christmas, my wife Helen enjoyed her usual
Westlife-fest. By the third playing of the song, I went
to bed, along with everyone else, leaving Hels dancing
by herself.

As I got to the bedroom, I decided to play a (slightly
immature) joke on Hels. I wrote a note saying I was
fed up, I'd had enough, I'd decided to leave and it was
all over.

I was just finishing the note when I heard Hels coming
up the stairs, so I put it on the side table and hid

under the bed. After a couple of moments, Hels stumbled into the bedroom, saw the note, picked it up and read it.

I was silently giggling to myself, until I heard the beeps of her mobile as she rang her best friend, Carolyn.

'Hello, darling. Did I wake you? Merry Christmas!' Then, she started laughing and I heard the words, 'Guess what, he's left me. I know. Isn't it great? I'm free.'

When she'd finished the call, she wandered out of the bedroom and down the stairs. I lay there under the bed for a few more moments in stunned silence, not knowing what to do. Eventually I came out of hiding and stood in the middle of the room, trembling. Adrenaline was coursing through me. I was in shock.

Looking over at the side table, I saw that Hels had added some words to the bottom of my note. I picked it up, and through teary eyes read, *I could see your feet, you idiot. Come downstairs and dance.*

Which I did.

Mum and Dad

HUGE THANKS TO...

Caspar, my friend and business mentor who has guided, encouraged and inspired me to become a speaker and to write this book. Thanks for all your support, mate.

Rhi, for her editing skills and excellent suggestions; Carolyn for her design work and unique sense of humour; Jules for putting up with Carolyn and sorting out the money; Bobby and Frank for their (gently put) criticisms and recommendations; Ali and John for their continued help and advice.

My family, for being the family anyone would want – Will and Ed, Alan, Faith, Kelly, Carla, Charlie, Rachel, Joe, Archie and Eva, plus the Watts gang scattered around the globe.

A special mention to Mum. This book focuses mainly on Dad – a remarkable man – but he'd have been lost without his wife. She was his rock and he adored her. She's also been an incredible mum, bringing up three demanding boys while forging her own highly successful career.

Finally, my boy Luke, whom I adore and who is my best teacher. I am extremely proud to be his dad. And my wife Hels, my best friend/life companion who puts up with my demands, ego, insecurities, moods, drama queen moments and odd quirks. You have my love and gratitude for ever.

THE AUTHOR

Nick Saunders

As a professional speaker, Nick speaks at all sorts of events, in all sorts of venues, in all sorts of countries.

He is best known for delivering keynote speeches at conferences where he encourages people to think, gets them to laugh and challenges them to change. He gets results.

Nick would be delighted to hear from you. Do get in touch.

e-mail: **nick@thefamilyman.co.uk**
or visit: **www.thefamilyman.co.uk**

SEE NICK IN ACTION

nick**saunders**
the family man

Do you work in an organisation where some people don't get on? Where there are personality clashes among certain individuals?

Nick Saunders, 'The Family Man', is the guy who fixes that by getting people to work together better, collaborate more, function effectively – all of which leads to improved performance and increased profit.

Nick relates his speeches to the organisation he is working with to ensure the message is pitched at exactly the right level. He will precisely tailor the content to your requirements. He turns relationships into results.

Lightning Source UK Ltd.
Milton Keynes UK
UKHW02f1735220318
319882UK00009B/141/P